MURDERS ON ALCATRAZ

GEORGE DEVINCENZI

ALCATRAZ
IS SPANISH
•FOR•
"PELICAN"

ALCATRAZ, CALIF.

To Will
Regards,
Geo. DeVincenzi
9-15-17

ISBN: 0692202285
ISBN 13: 9780692202289

CONTENTS

PREFACE

I wanted to write this book because of my experiences on Alcatraz. I have been giving speeches for twenty-five years and have been conducting night tours once a month for corporations for three years. My family and many friends have continuously persuaded me to write this book. Until now, I have not had enough enthusiasm to proceed. My son Mark and his wife, Nancy, have continuously encouraged me to write about my experiences for the last three years; I am attempting to fulfill their desires and mine.

There must be over fifty books written about Alcatraz. I have read almost all of them over the years, and I might add they are all very well done and interesting. Some depict the history of Alcatraz prior to its discovery by Spanish explorers while others concentrate on Alcatraz when it was a military disciplinary prison. Its buildings, gardens, and the San Francisco Bay surrounding the island have all been thoroughly explored and explained many times.

This book compiles actual experiences I have been involved in, and I kept it as simple and concise as possible while recounting details to the best of my memory. All the incidences described actually took place as stated and were brought forth to the best of my recollection.

I have been told that the following stories are exceptional and very interesting to all the people who have been listening to me over the last twenty-five years while giving tours at Alcatraz. I hope my efforts have been successful and you enjoy reading these historical stories I accumulated during my eight years as an officer on "the Rock."

WELCOME TO ALCATRAZ

My name is George DeVincenzi, and I was born in the Italian section of North Beach in San Francisco.

When I was a young boy/teenager, I used to sell newspapers, shine shoes, and fish along the docks in San Francisco. I was always fascinated by all the tourists at Fisherman's Wharf looking through telescopes at the federal penitentiary called Alcatraz. I myself used to put nickels and dimes in the telescope and watch, I was fascinated by what was going on the island. Never in a million years did I think I would be working there.

In 1944, at seventeen years old, I joined the US Navy. After sixteen months overseas, I returned home and found it extremely difficult to obtain employment anywhere. At that time, fifteen million servicemen were returning home and looking for work. I wanted to explore the possibilities of civil service. I decided to take federal, state, city, and county civil service examinations. I took the Alcatraz civil service test on a lark to see what it would be like. Low and behold, I must have passed with high grades because I was contacted immediately for an interview. I was intrigued by the prospect of going over to Alcatraz to see what it would be like. I was interviewed by at least three officials, taking up the better part of a whole day. Upon completion of a thorough examination, I took the boat home thinking that was the end of the process for hiring. Within the week, I was sent to Fort Mason, a substation of the Presidio in San Francisco for a physical examination, and I began to suspect they might want to hire me. I would say within the month, I received a telephone call from Alcatraz asking when I would be available to come to work. At this time, I was very surprised there was a strong possibility I would be working at Alcatraz.

I started to work within the month, and I went through four straight weeks of intensive preparation to become a correctional officer in the Federal Bureau of Prisons. My starting salary was three thousand dollars a year! The training course was very intense, consisting of lectures, movies, firearms training, hand-to hand combat, and daily testing on all aspects of being a correctional officer, eight hours a day. Upon completion of four weeks of training, which I felt was well prepared and thorough, I was told to take the weekend off and come to work the 9:00-to-5:30 shift the following Monday.

CHAPTER 1

MURDER IN THE BARBERSHOP

Monday morning at 0900, in a full pressed dress uniform, starched shirt, and shiny new shoes, I was locked into the barbershop with seven black inmates. The black barber, Inmate Freddy Lee Thomas (#893), began to cut Inmate Joseph Barsock's (#884) hair. They were speaking in low tones, almost whispering to each other. I became a little suspicious when the conversations got higher and higher in tone. Just then, Inmate Barsock jumped out of the chair, and Inmate Thomas lunged at him with a pair of seven-inch barber's shears. He stabbed him the heart, throat, and lungs, and I, like a damn fool, jumped in, trying to separate them while blowing the whistle. The three of us spun around, knocking over the second barber's chair, as Thomas continuously stabbed Barsock's body. In the ensuing battle/altercation, Thomas the barber accidentally cut my thigh. I sustained a cut about ten inches long. I landed on top of the two inmates and got possession of the barber's shears. I didn't know exactly how it happened at the time, but I ended up with the barber's shears in my hand. At this time, a very strange thing happened: while Barsock was lying in a large pool of blood, Inmate Thomas bent down and said, "I love you." Then, he kissed him on the face. The next moment, the barbershop door opened and three other officers rushed in to see what the altercation was all about.

This all occurred at 9:15 a.m. on my first day and first assignment. Lieutenant Bergen took the shears from me and said, "I have been in the prison service for many years, and I have never seen anyone get initiated as you were." He instructed me to go to the prison hospital and get my leg treated by the medical doctor. I was upset because I was wearing my new uniform and my new shoes were cut too!

Two FBI men immediately came to the island and interviewed me in the warden's office. We proceeded into the barbershop, and I had to explain what had happened. In the process, we examined the cabinet inside the barbershop, and hidden in a large stack of towels, we found a twelve-inch piece of glass with two inmates' socks, held with rubber bands, wrapped around it, creating a handle. Obviously, Thomas had intended to kill Barsock one way or another. Subsequently, electric clippers replaced scissors, which were never used again.

Consequently, I had to testify as a key witness at the murder trial, which was postponed once and lasted at least two weeks. Thomas received an additional thirty years. When Alcatraz closed in 1963, Thomas was transferred to a federal penitentiary in Leavenworth, Kansas, where another inmate murdered him.

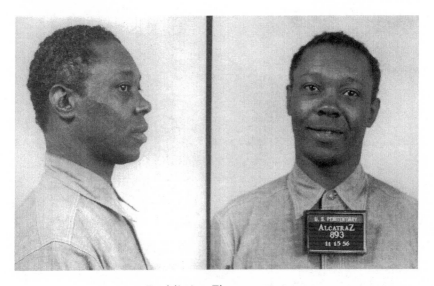

Freddie Lee Thomas #893

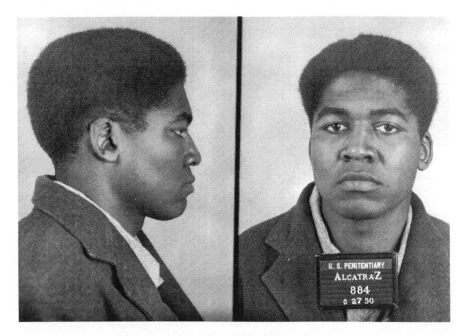

Joseph Barsock #884

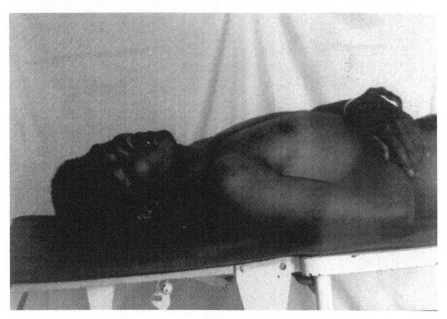

Barsock's dead body lying in hospital.

Died, May 28, 1951 about 10:30 a.m. from stab
wounds inflicted by Freddie Lee Thomas, #893-AZ

USP-AC Form 176

Name Joseph Barsock   **No.** 884-AZ **Color** Negro **Rec'd** June 27,1950 **From** McNeil Is.   **Date of Birth** Mar. 2, 1926   **Age**

Offense Murder on Gov't Property
Date of Sentence July 26, 1948
Sentence Life
Sentence began July 26, 1948
Minimum exp. date Life
Maximum exp. date
Parole date July 25, 1963

Good conduct credits
Credits forfeited
Credits restored

District sentenced S-CALIF. Los Angeles

DETAINERS none

Partners or co-defendants none

Reason For Transfer

This man has a civil life sentence which he is unable to accept. He is extremely reluctant to comply with institution rules and is not interested in a program for himself, giving expression to his feelings through rebelliousness. Because of long sentence and maladjustment Committee recommended transfer to Alcatraz

Former Institutional Rule Violations 14

10-15-48 Disobeyed officers order at steam table.
1-13-49 Took two cups of milk after told to take one.
4-15-49 Taking a handful of bacon and stealing cake.
4-26-49 Left crew, going to dish tank room, against rule
6-30-49 Left job in front of cannery, going to Power Hse
9-20-49 Playing cards in Hammock Hall, when cell is 4f2
9-29-49 In the wrong cell during evening count.
11-8-49 Taking a heavy undershirt to another prisoner
11-21-49 Sent to commissary when on restrictions.
1-23-50 Went to CH floor before crew called,missed crew.
2-21-50 Possession of 3 oz bottle of saccharine.
3-27-50 Received package of lye from another inmate
4-4-50 Mutilated pair of trousers and threw them to flo
4-10-50 Did not turn in pair of shorts at bath, had torn them and hid same in shoe, in cell.

Criminal History

12-10-47 PD-Long Beach, Calif. Susp. robbery. On 3-31-48, illegally wearing uniform & petty theft. Was given 6 months sentence, suspended and placed on probation for 3 yrs. Not likely to be wanted on account of long sentence

PRESENT CHARGE: Mar. 31, 1948, subject received six mos. sentence, suspended and 3 yrs probation for illegal wearing uniform and larceny on Govt. reservation. Approx. 2 a.m., Apr. 3, 1948, he was arrested wearing a Navy enlisted man's uniform at the U.S. Naval Station, Long Beach, Calif, on charges of false identification and theft. En route to the brig, Terminal Is., in custody of naval guard, subject overpowered guard, obtained is gun. While holding guard at bay with gun, turned and shot Navy Chief Petty Officer, Howard E. Jepson, who approached the scene when he heard the struggle between Barsock and the guard. Chief Jepson who, a few minutes previous had given subject a brief physical examination, died almost instantly. Barsock then ran and escaped the base and was found 10:a.m. same day hiding in a ship

Escape record or attempt to escape

Escaped from Terminal Island Navy Base while being taken to brig on minor offense, after shooting Chief Petty Officer.

Medical, Neuro-Psychiatrical, Educational, Religious, Social and Employments.

Good health; I.Q. 91, without mental disorder; claims 2 yrs high school but tests only 5th grade; Baptist religion; Born in New Orleans, La.; claims to be married with one child; does not know whereabouts of father; mother remarried and lives in New Orleans with stepfather of subject; ordinary laborer, roustabout.

Joseph Barsock #884 Prison Record

Where murder occurred on my first hour of my first day!

CHAPTER 2

MY SECOND MURDER
INMATE EDWARD HORACE GAUVIN #1134

Five years later, in 1955, I was promoted to senior officer. As a result, I was given more responsible positions, like hospital officer, cell-house in charge, treatment unit officer, clothing room officer, and control center officer. One particular morning, I was told I would be the acting lieutenant and was given instructions to get Inmate Edward Horace Gauvin (#1134) out of the D Block Treatment Unit and get him prepared for return to the general population within the prison. Inmate Gauvin had been confined to segregation in D Block for over two years. D Block was a separate area for inmates who needed to be confined away from the general prison population. He was there to protect his life from another inmate. I proceeded with two other officers to D Block and escorted Inmate Gauvin to the clothing room one floor below where all the inmates showered. At this point, unfortunately for Gauvin, Inmate Ronald Eugene Simcox (#1131) had been assigned to work in the clothing room. Simcox was an ex-army inmate doing forty years for mutiny. He had a shiv (knife) concealed somewhere, and he attacked Gauvin, stabbing him to death while he was stepping in to take a shower. We immediately went to Gauvin's assistance, but it was too late. He died almost instantly. At this point, I was beginning to wonder why I had ever taken this position at Alcatraz.

Mug Shot of Roland Simcox #1131

George DeVincenzi with inmate Simcox and
U. S. Deputy Marshall going to trial for murder charge in 1955.

CHAPTER 3

ROBERT STROUD, BIRDMAN OF ALCATRAZ, #594

Robert Franklin Stroud born January 28, 1890, was a federal American prisoner, cited as one of the most notorious criminals in American history. During his time at Leavenworth Penitentiary he reared and sold birds and became a respected ornithologist, but despite his nickname, he was not permitted to keep his birds at Alcatraz where he was incarcerated from 1942. Born in Seattle, Stroud ran away from his abusive father at the age of 13, and by the time he was 18, he had become a pimp in Alaska. In January 1909,he shot and killed a barman who had attacked one of his prostitutes, Kitty O'Brien. He turned himself into authorities. He was found guilty of manslaughter on the 23rd of August 1909, and sentenced to 12 years in the Federal Penitentiary on Puget Sound's McNeil Island. Stroud gained a reputation as an extremely dangerous inmate who frequently had confrontations with fellow inmates. Stroud began serving his life sentence in solitary confinement at Leavenworth Prison, where in 1920, while walking in the prison recreation yard he discovered a nest with three injured sparrows in the recreation yard. He began raising them and within a few years he had a collection of 300

Canaries. He began extensive research in studying Canaries after being granted equipment by a radical prison reforming warden, and published "Diseases of Canaries" in 1933. The book was smuggled out of Leavenworth and sold in masses, and a later edition "Stroud's Digest On the Diseases of Birds" in 1943. Stroud ran a successful business from within the prison making concoctions to cure the birds diseases. His birding activities infuriated prison staff because of his ongoing demands relative to caring for his birds. He was constantly asking for ice, chemicals, bird seed, materials to build cages and this was annoying to prison officials. Due to the acquisition of chemicals, he was secretly able to make distilled alcohol for his own consumption. Due to his constant abuse of prison rules, mainly alcohol, he was transferred to Alcatraz.

There is a misconception that Robert Stroud had birds on Alcatraz. This never happened. He kept his birds while in captivity in Leavenworth Penitentiary. When he was transferred to Alcatraz on December 19, 1942, he had to relinquish all aspects of his bird business because this was strictly prohibited. He began serving his life sentence while at Alcatraz.

When I first went to Alcatraz as a new officer, every Saturday morning, my duty was to go with another officer to the hospital and supervise Robert's bath. This lasted for six months. It was the warden's instructions that any time Robert was removed from his cell, every other inmate in the hospital, including orderlies, janitors, and so on, had to be locked up before we could remove him from his cell. This was strictly enforced by the warden because Robert was a high-risk prisoner. In 1943, Robert was diagnosed as a sociopath with an IQ of 134. He had committed two previous murders; one of his victims was a guard at Leavenworth, Kansas. He stabbed the guard to death in the main dining room of the prison in front of two thousand witnesses. I would give Robert a locked razor, and he would shave his face, head, and whole body. A locked razor required an Allen wrench tool to remove and replace the blade. He would then take a bath in the physical therapy room across the hall from his cell, which he loved to do, and this would require considerable time, thereby infringing on my lunch hour. I used to say, "Robert, get out of there. I have to go to lunch."

He would say, "Please give me a few more minutes."

Naturally, I let him stay a few minutes longer. While I was doing this, the other officer would be in Stroud's cell shaking it down thoroughly, looking for any contraband, such as concealed prescribed drugs, which he had attempted to use for suicide purposes on two occasions. Upon completion of his bath, he would be given a complete set of new socks and underwear and new bedding. We would lock him back in his cell, and the hospital would resume its normal activities.

Over the years, I was the hospital officer for approximately eighteen months on three different shifts, and I got to know Stroud very well. I am not proud to admit this, but I used to play checkers with him on the twelve-to-eight morning shift occasionally. The only time I would do this was if I knew the gun gallery officer, who could look through a peephole to make sure I was safe. If I knew the gun gallery officer and trusted him, I would play checkers in front of Stroud's cell at 2:00 or 3:00 in the morning. Altogether, I played numerous checker games with him and don't believe I ever won a game! If I did not know the gun gallery officer and could not trust him, I would never do this. I would open the heavy wood door in front of his barred cell door and place a small table and stool with a checkerboard on the table. If I had been caught by the administration doing this, I could have been fired immediately. However, I had the key that allowed me to prevent anyone from entering the hospital. In the same time frame, Stroud was studying Spanish, Latin, and French. He knew I was an Italian and always tried to speak Italian with me, but he was not very proficient with his Italian and was constantly butchering the language. I would try to correct him, but we never got too far! He would always ask me questions about my family, but because of proper training in regards to officers becoming too familiar with inmates, I discouraged any further inquiries about my personal life. This was strictly enforced by the prison administration policies at all times.

He read books and magazines continuously and would sleep on and off throughout the day and stay awake the better part of the night reading. On the exterior of the main cell house, it had large extending arms holding illuminating lamps that light up the whole exterior surface. From the lamps he would be able to see and read all night!

He continuously tried to get people to talk to him while looking through the glass. He was a great admirer of the Jesuit priest Father Richard Scanell and would stand in front of the glass looking for Father Scanell as he walked by. Father had many duties to perform while in the hospital, and Stroud would try to monopolize all his time. Father, knowing this, would duck down as he walked by Stroud's door to avoid his notice and continue down the hall so he could perform his priestly duties. Upon departing the hospital, Father had to duck down again so Robert would not see him. At this point, Robert would try to get my attention and ask me what had happened to Father Scanell. I would reply, "I will make sure he comes to see you when he gets here." He would visit Robert once a week, depending on his schedule, during his five-year tenure as the priest on the island.

Father Scanell was highly regarded as a Jesuit priest. He served Mass on the island for the civilians and tended to the needs of the prisoners. I often think of him as a true friend and a scholar. He also taught classes at the University of San Francisco.

Elizabeth Stroud, Robert's mother, started a massive letter-writing campaign. She wrote to President Wilson and asked him to commute his sentence from death to life in solitary confinement. On April 15, 1920, five days before he was to be executed by hanging, Robert was sentenced to solitary confinement for the rest of his life without the possibility of parole. Solitary confinement meant he could never be with the general population within Alcatraz and had to be confined by himself, never allowed to speak to or associate with any other inmates.

In February of 1963 Stroud met and talked with actor Burt Lancaster, who portrayed him in the movie "The Birdman of Alcatraz". It should be noted that Stroud never got to see the movie or read the book that was based on his life.

Robert was in prison for over fifty years. If you are interested in his life and want to learn more about him, there are many books about his life. On November 21, 1963, Robert Franklin Stroud died at the Springfield Medical center at the age of 73. Robert is buried next to his Mother in Metropolis, Illinois. He was incarcerated the last 54 years of his life, of which 42 were spent in solitary confinement.

Alcatraz mug shot

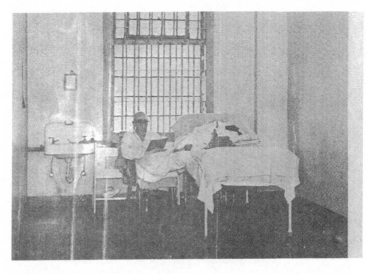

Rare photo of Robert Stoud reading in his cell

CHAPTER 4

WILLIAM EDWARD COOK JUNIOR #710 (BILLY COOK): THREE HUNDRED YEARS FOR MURDER AND KIDNAPPING

Of all the inmates I was involved with on Alcatraz, I honestly believe that Billy Cook is the one I despised the most. I recall he had the words "Hard Luck" tattooed on his fingers.

He started out in Tulsa, Oklahoma, and traveled up to Missouri. In 1951, he killed a mother and father and three children and dropped them into a deep well in Tulsa Oklahoma. After terrorizing Southern California and killing seven people, he fled into Mexico, murdered a man, stole his automobile, shot him and stuffed him into a trunk. He then kidnapped two prospectors from California and took their 1949 Studebaker. Mexican officials received a tip that Cook and his two captives were seen in Santa Rosales, 200 miles South East of the Peninsula. Two hours later, Mexican officers spotted Cook getting out of the car and arrested him. He surrendered without any resistance. . From Missouri to California, I believe the record will show he killed eight people and kidnapped three. Unfortunately, one was a Deputy Sheriff from Southern California. He was given three hundred years (six fifty-year sentences) and sentenced to Alcatraz in 1951. I never liked him personally. He spit in my face once when I told him to clean up his cell. He would never speak to anyone, and, believe it or not, he used to sit in his cell and read the Bible. Because he killed a deputy sheriff from Southern California, the federal government released him to the State of California to be transferred to San Quentin for execution on December 12, 1952. Due to the notoriety of the case, I had the day off, so I went to San Quentin with coworkers and saw Billy Cook be executed in the gas chamber. This is not a pleasant experience to observe but definitely warranted with this particular inmate.

Inmate Cook received the longest specific sentence ever given to an Alcatraz inmate.

Inmate Billy Cook #710.

CHAPTER 5

MORTON SOBELL #996, THE SPY

Morton Sobell was a coconspirator with Mr. and Mrs. Rosenberg in the late forties and early fifties, and he and the Rosenbergs were given the death penalty in Sing Sing prison in New York for espionage. Mr. and Mrs. Rosenberg were directly responsible for stealing the atomic bomb secrets from the United States and giving them to Russia. This was a highly publicized trial at the time that resulted in them getting the death penalty. Inmate Morton Sobell was given thirty years because there was not sufficient evidence to warrant the death penalty. He was therefore sent directly to Alcatraz on November 26, 1952, where he was serving his sentence. Morton was one of only three or four prisoners sent directly to Alcatraz from the courts. He was sent to Alcatraz because of the notoriety of the case, which included global ramifications. In 2008, Morton Sobell directly admitted in an interview with the *New York Times* that he did turn over secrets to the Soviet Union.

Morton Sobell was a highly educated electrical engineer and knew how to do Alcatraz time. He kept to himself during his seventeen years at Alcatraz, did not associate with other inmates openly, and never got into any serious trouble.

His wife would fly out from New York to San Francisco once a month; she would come on the last day of the month and the first day of the following month. By this arrangement, she could visit two consecutive days. Ten years ago, I revealed to the public, while speaking to the visitors on Alcatraz, she exposed her breast to her husband while visiting. Being a good officer and observing everything that took place within sight and hearing, I had to do my job and watch this all unfold! Since then, Morton Sobell has been asked by numerous people about this incident and readily admits that it did happen.

Prior to 1963, when Alcatraz closed, Sobell was transferred to the medical facility for federal prisoners in Springfield, Missouri. There in Springfield, Missouri, he became close friends with Robert Stroud. In January 1965, Sobell was transferred to Lewisburg, Pennsylvania, and was finally released on January 14, 1969.

In conclusion, I never appreciated any American citizen who would conspire against his or her own government and get involved in an incident like this. This was a highly celebrated case in 1951, because it was so unusual for an American to be convicted of spying. President Truman and Eisenhower turned down their appeal for clemency, and Mr. and Mrs. Rosenberg were executed by electrocution at the Sing Sing prison on June 19, 1953. Ethel Rosenberg was thirty-seven years old. Julius Rosenberg was thirty-five.

Morton Sobell #996.

CHAPTER 6

JIMMY GROVE #158, A VERY DANGEROUS INMATE

One prisoner, Jimmy Grove, made a lasting impression on me. Even to this day, I think of him often. A very sad case and beginning for a human being who was raised by foster parents, ran away from home at age 12, convicted two years later for burgulary and received three years in Missouri State Reformatory. At the age of nineteen, again convicted of robbery he was sent to a Utah state prison. He also did time at Walla Walla State Prison for a burgulary conviction. He was allowed to join the United States Army even with three prison sentences. He was charged with attempting to rape a ten year old girl, daughter of an Army officer. He received a twenty year sentence and sent to Fort Leavenworth prison. Grove went from bad to worse, fighting with other prisoners and he stabbed another black inmate and received another twenty years. At Leavenworth penitentiary he continued this behavior fighting withother inmates and attempted suicide twice.

He arrived on Alcatraz September 4, 1934. Jimmy, who was African American, was notorious for not getting along with other black inmates on Alcatraz because they were afraid of him. He was doing time for murder and had attacked and stabbed numerous other inmates while confined on the island. He was sent to solitary and segregation forty-four times. When I was working the midnight to 8:00 a.m. shift, I was the cell house officer at the west end. I used to get sleepy and tired working this particular shift, and at times,

I would doze off for a few seconds. Jimmy Grove was celled above me to my immediate left in the first cell of the second tier. He would get a page or two from a legal pad, crumple it up, throw it at me, and hit my desk to wake me up. He would say, "Look out; the lieutenant is coming in soon." I thought this was quite unique because he was considered one of the worst and most dangerous inmates on Alcatraz. I would think to myself, *My God, here is one of the most dangerous inmates on Alcatraz, and he is looking out for me!* Eventually, when Alcatraz closed, he was sent to Atlanta, Georgia, and committed suicide there.

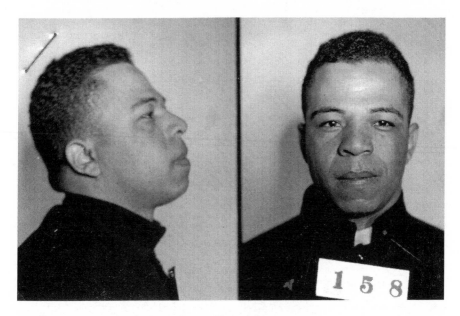

Jimmy Grove #158.

CHAPTER 7

OFFICER FISHER ATTACKED BY INMATE WILLARD MCKINNEY #931

Inmate Willard McKinney was the type of inmate at Alcatraz who disliked all prison authorities, had trouble getting along with officers, and was the sort who would lose control and become very dangerous.

It was the Warden's requirement that as all inmates were entering the dining room for breakfast, lunch, and dinner, they have their shirt collars and sleeves buttoned up. This particular day, I was the junior officer working with Senior Officer Fisher at the west end of the cell house leading into the dining room. Inmate McKinney, thirty years old and serving a twenty-year murder sentence, was entering the dining room, when Officer Fisher told him to button up his shirt and sleeves. McKinney turned around and cussed out Officer Fisher. Upon conclusion of the breakfast, as Inmate McKinney was returning to his cell, Officer Fisher told him to stay in his cell, as he was on report and being written up. Inmate McKinney went to his cell, picked up his trumpet,(he played the Trumpet in the prison band), and proceeded right by me up to the desk where Officer Fisher was getting ready to take the official count. He took a violent swing at Officer Fisher's head with the trumpet and struck him above the left ear. Blood spurted everywhere, and the officers rushed to subdue Inmate McKinney and assist Officer Fisher. McKinney was tried, convicted, and given five years and confined to segregation for many years.

Officer Fisher was partially paralyzed and to my recollection was never gainfully employed after this episode. He had sustained a fractured skull.

Inmate McKinney, a former Golden Gloves Boxer, was committed to Alcatraz for the 1944 shooting and killing of an army sergeant at Camp Patrick Henry Virginia. After having been shifted from one Federal Prison to another, McKinney was sent to Alcatraz in May 1951.

CHAPTER 8

CLARENCE CARNES #714, FULL-BLOODED CHOCTAW INDIAN FROM OKLAHOMA

Clarence was born in 1927 in Daisy Oklahoma, the oldest of four children. At sixteen years of age, Clarence was convicted of first-degree murder for the killing of a garage attendant during an attempted hold-up. He was sent to prison for life. After serious disciplinary problems and an escape from Leavenworth, he was sentenced to Alcatraz and arrived on July 1945. He was the youngest inmate to serve time on the Rock. At that time, he was only eighteen years of age and still serving his life sentence. Clarence was in and out of trouble the entire time he was at Alcatraz. While at Alcatraz he was assessed by psychiatrist Romney M. Ritchey and found to have a psychopathic personality, and to be emotionally unstable with an I.Q. of 93. He was directly involved in the large prison break of 1946. Three inmates were murdered during this prison break.

This particular morning, I was standing with my back against the wall facing B Block, waiting for the morning count to be completed. Low and behold, a paper kite came sailing down from the third tier of B Block and went scooting by me ten or twelve feet. I picked it up and read it: "Carnes has a knife and was going to kill Inmate Johnson." It did not indicate his first name or number; that was important, as we had numerous inmates with the name Johnson in the prison population. I immediately gave the note to Lieutenant

Severson, and he said, "when we open that tier, make sure Inmate Carnes's cell stays closed." Upon completion of letting all the inmates out so they could go to work, everything became quiet, and Lieutenant Serverson, two other officers, and I opened Carnes's cell. We physically searched him and found a copper knife approximately six inches long on his person. Consequently, we transported him to D Block and he was placed in isolation.

The metal detector machine could not pick up copper, brass, or glass objects. Objects inmates tried to manufacture out of these materials could not be detected. As a result, officers had to perform body and cell searches.

Whoever directed this message in kite form saved an inmate named Johnson's life. We were never able to determine which inmate named Johnson Carnes was trying to kill.

Inmate Clarence Carnes was spared the death penalty because he had refused to murder several guards he had been assigned to kill in the 1946 prison riot. During this riot, three inmates died and were later found in the B Block corridor.

In the early 1980's Carnes was working at a tourist shop near Fisherman's Wharf, meeting the public and talking about his experiences. I was working as a Customs Inspector on Pier 44, a short distance away. I made an effort to meet him at the Tourist Book Store and we had coffee and talked for over two hours. He was always cordial and never showed any animosity towards me.

Clarence Carnes #714.

CHAPTER 9

OFFICER PEPPER

Officer Pepper, a former professional boxer, who had a pushed-in nose and cauliflower ears, was somewhat of a character. He mostly worked in Towers and Gun Galleries. One particular night, I believe he may have had a couple of glasses of wine while playing cards before he went to work. He was stationed in the road tower from midnight to 8:00 in the morning. It was customary during the course of the evening shifts for the lieutenant on duty to roam all over the island, and when approaching a tower, he would flash his flashlight at the officer. It was necessary for the officer to acknowledge the lieutenant by returning the flashlight signal. This particular night, as the lieutenant was exiting the work area, he continuously flashed Officer Pepper in the road tower and never got a response. He worked himself closer and closer to the tower, continuously flashing the officer but still receiving no response. As he approached the tower entrance, he shook the outer door, and still there was no sign of Officer Pepper. He then walked all the way up to the cell house control center, approximately 250 yards, and picked up the key to enter the road tower from the control center officer. He walked all the way back to the road tower, again flashing Officer Pepper without a response. He entered the road tower proper and to make matters worse, after finding Officer Pepper asleep, he observed that he had removed his carbine rifle and placed it in the rack instead of carrying it at all times on his person. The lieutenant picked up the firearm, locked the door, and walked back to the cell house. He then called Officer Pepper and asked him for the serial number on his firearm. You can imagine Officer Pepper's surprise and reaction when he could not find his firearm. The lieutenant told him to stay awake and he would be replaced as soon as possible. Another officer was contacted, and within the hour, Officer Pepper was replaced and put on report. He was originally given thirty days off and could have been fired that day. With his many years of service, he was given an official reprimand and his sentence was reduced to fourteen days.

I was working at the main gate the night this all unfolded and was aware of all the intricate details.

Road Tower

CHAPTER 10

INMATE JOHN ELGIN JOHNSON #631, THE PLUMBER

Prior to Johnson's arrival at Alcatraz, he was incarcerated at Leavenworth Prison for bank robberies and an assault on a prison guard. I had Inmate Johnson as the cell house plumber for three months. Johnson was doing nine years (1944 to 1953) on Alcatraz for his crimes. On every job that he worked, I would accompany and supervise him. He was not a serious problem as an inmate. He never got into any trouble and served Mass every Sunday as the altar boy for Father Scannell. Father went to bat for Johnson and wrote a letter on his behalf, and eventually, he was released from Alcatraz and went to Los Angeles, the city of his choosing. At that time, it was necessary for him to register with the Los Angeles Parole Board. He had a form of trade since he had learned plumbing and machine-shop work in prison. In his own words, he learned to hate while at Alcatraz, which led to deviant behavior after his release from prison.

In 1953, in a Los Angeles suburb, he was a suspect in the strangulation and murder of one Richard Fagner, who had befriended him. While talking in a phone booth in the Baltimore, Maryland, town theater, he fired through the glass door fatally wounding an FBI agent named Murphy and seriously wounding another FBI man. Johnson died in the phone booth in the mezzanine of the theater under a hail of bullets from the FBI.

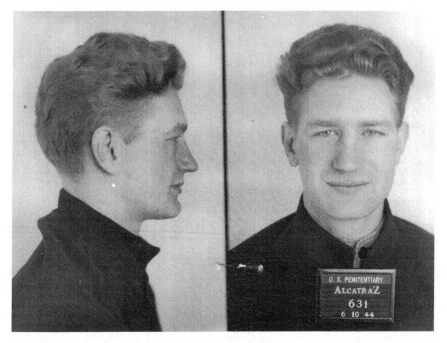

Inmate John E. Johnson #631.

CHAPTER 11

THE CLOSING OF THE GOLDEN GATE BRIDGE

I was assigned to the dock tower on the midnight-to-eight shift on December 1, 1951. On that particular day, San Francisco was hit by a terrific storm with winds approaching a hundred miles an hour. The rain and wind forced the closure of the Golden Gate Bridge for the first time since it was completed in 1937. The winds violently shook the Guard tower, which was sixty feet off the ground. The water in the toilet was swirling, and the whole tower was creaking and shaking. I telephoned Lieutenant Mahan and explained the situation I was in. I thought the tower could topple over and I would land in the bay in this steel enclosure. I found out later he was very busy tending to other emergencies on the island due to the inclement weather. Lieutenant Mahan did not respond to my calls, and I gave up trying to reach him again after the second time. Needless to say, I earned my salary that night and was happy as hell to be relieved at 8:00 a.m.

Golden Gate Bridge

Road Tower

CHAPTER 12

THREE-STAR ARMY
GENERAL SWING

This particular morning, I was a boat operator for the boat named *The Warden Johnson*. The boat was named after the first warden of Alcatraz who served from 1934 until 1948. His nickname was "Old Saltwater." As the boat officer, I tied the boat up to the pier on arrival and departure while helping each passenger when he or she stepped on and off the vessel. I paid particular attention to helping the children so they would not fall into the bay. This boat accommodated all visitors, children going to and coming home from school, and the residents who resided on Alcatraz. I noticed this morning we had two distinguished-looking passengers. One was Three-Star United States Army General Swing, and the other was his guest, a Two-Star Army General, whose name I did not know.

General Swing was a close personal friend of President Eisenhower; he had graduated from West Point with the president. Later, I learned that due to their close relationship, he was promoted to Commander in Chief of the Presidio in San Francisco.

As the boat departed to Alcatraz, we encountered inclement weather with excessive wind and choppy waters. The two Generals were standing up on the rear of the vessel in violation of the rules, which stated everyone should be seated. They both ignored my request to be seated.

General Swing was pointing out the scenic views of San Francisco to the other general. Just then, a gust of wind blew General Swing's gold-encrusted hat right off his head and into the bay. The hat was headed toward the Golden Gate Bridge. I got the impression General Swing was very embarrassed. He looked frustrated. I thought this was humorous because I had told him to stay seated and he completely ignored me.

General Swing was on the island four to five hours touring the prison that day, looking somewhat odd without his gold-encrusted hat on. I can imagine how he felt because the Two-Star General who accompanied him had his hat and was in his complete full-dress uniform.

I would guess a general's hat with all that gold braid would cost a couple of hundred dollars even in the 1950s.

CHAPTER 13

THE MCGARY INCIDENT

Inmate Leroy Mcgary (#712) was a large, muscular African American who had a history of mental problems and was confined in the flats of the segregation unit of D Block. He was constantly screaming and hollering, disrupting the whole D Block unit. You could even hear him in the cell house. Lieutenant Faulk, two other officers, and I had to enter his cell and subdue him to get him ready to be placed in isolation. He was very violent and combative, and we had to use physical force to subdue him for our own protection. It was prohibited to use a "sap," which resembled a leather-covered billy club, but in this situation, it was necessary because Inmate Mcgary was very combative and we had to protect ourselves. During this physical tussle, I was trying to hit Mcgary and I accidentally struck Lieutenant Faulk on his right hand and broke two of his fingers. In the ensuing battle, Inmate Mcgary took a violent swing, trying to hit me in the face. Luckily, I jumped back and he hit me in the chest, knocking me back about five feet. This caused a contusion on my chest wall that took a few days to heal.

Inmate Mcgary was eventually transferred to the federal medical facility at Springfield, Missouri, due to his mental health issues.

Years later, after Lieutenant Faulk passed on, I told Mrs. Faulk about this unfortunate incident, and she readily remembered him having difficulty with his hand and broken fingers.

I would like to explain it was not the policy of the Federal Bureau of Prisons to use extensive force unless it was necessary to protect us under these trying conditions.

D Block: Segregation and Isolation

CHAPTER 14

THE IMPRISONED SEA GULL

At the conclusion of the last boat arriving to the island for the day, which was around 1:00 a.m., the boat officer's duty was to patrol the entire island, which took about two hours, while focusing on the industry building. Duties consisted of fire patrol and shaking down inmates' work areas and looking for contraband. There were many nights when the wind would be blowing, there would be heavy fog and poor visibility, and temperatures would get down into the thirties. With rain, trying to walk on the uneven, hilly terrain throughout the island was a challenge. Upon completion of this patrol, the officer was subject to assisting the lieutenant on duty, helping the control officer on duty if necessary, and being the main gate officer for the remainder of the shift.

One particular day, I was working the midnight-to-eight shift, and upon arrival of the last boat to Alcatraz, at approximately 1:00 a.m., my job was to completely circle the entire island myself armed with a flashlight, checking for contraband and fires possibly set by inmates. I had to work around the edge of the island to the industry building, which was located at the far end of the island. I opened a large door that gave me entrance to the industry building. As I opened the door, a sea gull flew directly at me, squawking and flapping its wings. It flew right over my head out the door. At that point, I thought I was going to have a heart attack. The bird had been accidentally locked in at the conclusion of the day shift around 4:30 p.m. Today as I visit the Island and see and hear the Sea Gulls squawking, I always reflect on that incident and smile about it!

Attacking Seagull

CHAPTER 15

THE HAIRCUTS IN D BLOCK

My first six months of employment as a correctional officer on Alcatraz, I was assigned to be the barbershop officer. It was my job as the officer to supervise the activity in the barbershop. I became familiar with the white inmates' barber, Inmate Wagner #911, who cut all the white inmates' hair. I believe he was a professional barber from Kansas City, Missouri, before he became an inmate at the Rock. During this time, there were black barbers appointed for black inmates and white barbers for white inmates. I watched on a daily basis as Inmate Wagner gave haircuts to the various inmates. When the inmates were assigned to D Block, segregation and isolation, they could not leave their cells for twenty-four hours. I was asked by the captain to go into D Block for two straight days for about four hours each day and cut inmates' hair using only electric clippers and combs. As a new officer, I thought this was a peculiar assignment because I had no knowledge of cutting hair and had my own doubts about how well I would perform. Apparently, I did a good job because some inmates told me their haircuts were adequate and some of the inmates gave me a bad time while I was giving them haircuts and in a humorous manner teased me frequently.

About five years later, I was sitting with a friend of mine at the Lost Weekend Cocktail Lounge on Taraval Street in San Francisco having a cocktail. The bartender came up to me with a drink and said, "This is from the gentleman at the end of the bar." I looked up, and low and behold, there was Inmate Wagner, the white inmate barber who taught me everything I know about cutting hair. I immediately went up to him, and we renewed old acquaintances. He apparently was discharged from Leavenworth prison after completing his sentence two years prior. I bought him a drink, and we had a long discussion about our prior Alcatraz experiences.

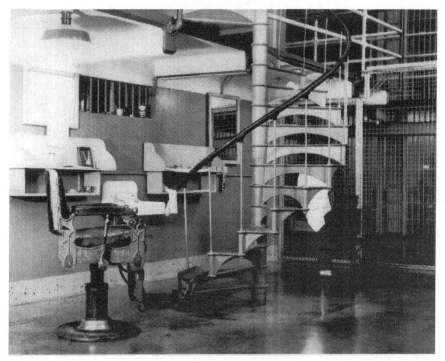

Photo of Barber Shop and Barber Chair

CHAPTER 16

SERIOUS CULINARY STRIKE

Within the first six months of my assignment, we had a serious culinary strike in the kitchen that lasted approximately three weeks. The inmates who worked in the kitchen did not like the quality or quantity of the food and initiated the strike. The stewards did not manage their kitchen responsibilities adequately, which included ordering and purchasing food for the prison population. The Associate Warden directed twenty-five inmates to go to D Block, segregation. I can remember seeing five inmates in one cell for two days. Due to the overcrowding in D Block, it was necessary to transfer twenty-five inmates to A Block. A Block had not been used since it was an army prison from 1907 to 1933 because it was never modernized like B, C, and D Blocks. B, C, and D Blocks had tool-proof steel, which meant the inmates could not cut through the bars. The lieutenant approached me at 10:00 in the morning and said, "Would you mind going home and getting some rest and returning at midnight to take over A Block?" This meant working in A Block from midnight to 8:00 a.m. the following morning.

I came to work that night, and during the course of the evening, an inmate on the second tier broke an incandescent light bulb and slashed his throat with the broken glass. I had to call the lieutenant and a medical technician. The inmate was transported to the hospital for medical attention. A Block was closed permanently after this strike was over. I remember when the whole prison had to be fed sandwiches in their cells instead of going to the dining room in order to bring the strike to a halt. It required getting inmate volunteers and some officers to prepare sandwiches to overcome the strike.

37

End of C Block cells

Top tier of Broadway Cells

Times Square: Got it's nick name from the clock on the wall.

Recreation Yard wall and the Road tower, with the
Golden Gate Bridge in the distance.

The boat Warden Johnson

George DeVincenzi 1950's

Inmates filing into Mess hall.
Notice tear gas canisters above

Officer Rayle: Supervising the Recreation Yard.

Broadway Cells at night.

Broadway-Main Cell Block Aisle.

AZ Aerial photo of Alcatraz taken in 1934.

Typical Alcatraz Cell.

Photo of Postmistress Mrs. Jean Long and her children arriving on the island circa: 1950's. Mrs. Long was the wife of correctional officer Bill Long.

Reunion photo of George DeVincenzi and former inmate Bob Luke on Alcatraz

Photo of command center

Photo of Alcatraz Towers

Alcatraz Card

ALcatraz Cottages

Alcatraz from Fishermans Wharf

George 1946

George 2012

George & Guards

George Early 1950

George in Cell

End of C Block Cells

Alcatraz Vintage Fire Truck 1934

Guard At Work

Guard Poster

Young George in Lower Left Side of Photo

Guard Reunion

Lecture on Alatraz

Presentation on Alcatraz for Special Event

Officer Rayle in Rec Yard

Pelican

Rec Yard

Road Tower

Visitors Talking To Inmates

Typical Cell

USF Basketball players Bill Russel and Casey Jones, University
of San Francisco Basketball Players Visiting Alcatraz

Famous View Alcatraz Sign at Fisherman's Wharf

Warden Johnson

Young George

CHAPTER 17

ABE "THE TRIGGER MAN" CHALUPOWITZ

Abe "the Trigger" Chapman (Chalupowitz) was a small man in physical appearance, with a very heavy reputation. I believe he is written about in *Murder Incorporated* as one of many triggermen. He is reported to have assassinated twelve individuals. Murder Incorporated was an organization that terrorized the East Coast for many years, killing a thousand people from 1920 to 1940. The killings were done for the preservation of the vast business interests of the Rackets. Abe had the first cell in the flats of C Block as you entered the cell house through the main gate.

When I was the East End Cell House Officer, I used to converse with him quite frequently through the course of a quiet day. He had a slight Russian accent that I detected when we spoke to each other. He was always pleasant, and I enjoyed talking with him because he was interesting. One day, upon reading about him, I discovered his sordid background. He left Alcatraz and was transferred to Atlanta, Georgia, from where he was apparently paroled.

One day, in 1953, when I was off, I was at a new shopping mall on Bay Street having lunch at a fish and chips restaurant. I felt a tap on my shoulder, and there to my surprise was Chalupowitz saying hello to me. I found out during our conversation that he was half owner of the restaurant and wanted to know if I had paid for my lunch. He offered to reimburse me, but I refused. We spoke for another hour reviewing our Alcatraz experiences.

Can you imagine an Alcatraz ex-inmate with his reputation, sitting down with me and sharing lunch? I often think of Chalupowitz trying to buy my lunch after all those years.

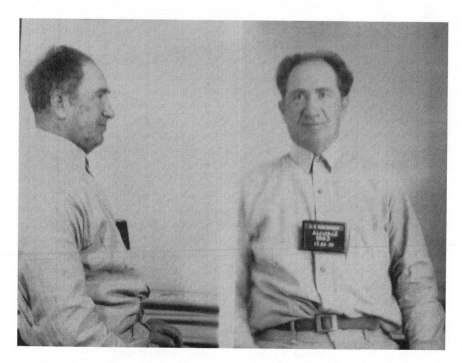

Abe Chalupowitz #1043

CHAPTER 18

HOSPITAL "BUG JUICE"

When I first came to work on Alcatraz, I realized that there was a serious drug problem in the hospital. Every evening, before bedtime, around twelve to fifteen inmates would line up in the large hospital ward and wait to get a small cup of "Bug Juice." Bug Juice was a narcotic used for sleeping purposes. It consisted of a thick, white substance of syrup consistency that was served in a small white cup. The Bug Juice created problems with many inmates trying to enter the hospital so they could obtain the narcotic for sleep. I can recall inmates cutting themselves on their arms and legs in order to gain access to the hospital. The problem persisted, and eventually, Doctor Meltzer, who was an MD and psychiatrist, was transferred to Alcatraz to solve this problem. When Alcatraz tried to cut back on the use of this narcotic, many inmates got into fights and physically abused themselves so they could have the Bug Juice for sleep.

One day, while I was walking down Broadway (the main walkway leading toward the kitchen separating B and C Blocks, Inmate Arnold Kyle (#547) while in his cell in the kitchen row, called me to show me he had cut his arms from wrists to elbows. He was bleeding profusely. I immediately called the lieutenant to notify him, and Kyle was escorted to the hospital for treatment. This was a common occurrence. The administration tried to solve the problem over the next two years and ultimately did. Dr. Meltzer drastically cut back on the use of narcotics for sleep even if the inmate purposely cut himself for entry into the hospital. Inmate Kyle, who was the brother-in-law of Joseph Paul Cretzer, a notorious inmate, was shot dead in the 1946 prison riot at Alcatraz.

At a Alcatraz reunion about 5 years ago, I was happy to see Doctor Meltzer again after all these years. He remembered me right away and said he was going to write a book and wanted my phone number to concur with me about the drug problem we had at the hospital. Unfortunately I never heard from him to this day.

Arnold Kyle # 547

CHAPTER 19

INMATE JOHN GUIDO IOZZI, #1197

I can remember reading in John Guido Iozzi's professional file in 1954 that he had knocked out his first twelve professional fights before he became incarcerated. I also saw a photo in the *New York Times* of Jack Dempsey with his arm around Iozzi. Mr. Dempsey stated: "I believe Iozzi could be the next heavyweight champion of the world." Jack Dempsey held the World Heavyweight Championship from 1919 to 1926.

He was arrested for stealing an automobile. He crossed over the state line, which made this crime a federal offense. Iozzi was sentenced for one to three years in a federal prison. Due to his personality, he got into fights and escaped, and eventually, I believe, he got five years and was transported to Alcatraz.

At this point, being a disruptive inmate, he eventually worked himself into D Block and was placed in the segregation cells. The D Block consisted of segregation and isolation.

While in one of the isolation cells, being in a frenzied state of mind, instead of using the toilet facility, which consisted of a hole in the corner of the cell, he intentionally defecated on the floor of the cell. I find it difficult to describe what took place, but he proceeded to throw his feces at the wall and wrote obscenities with them. He cussed out the Warden, Captain, and other Officers. I had the misfortune of having to go in with two other officers to quiet him down by using force. Upon completion, I was politely told to clean myself up and put on a clean uniform.

I often thought how ridiculous the situation with Iozzi was at that time. He started out with a comparatively minor crime of stealing a car, and because he was such a disruptive inmate, he consequently worked himself up to Alcatraz.

D Block
Showing separation and isolation cells.

CHAPTER 20

WARDEN SWOPE

Warden Edward B. Swope was the warden when I arrived as a correctional officer on Alcatraz. He had a very serious reputation as a tough and strict disciplinarian. He was the Warden from 1948 to 1955 and was disliked by most correctional officers and many residents of the island. Swope owned a dog, an Irish Setter, but did not allow anyone else on the island to have a dog. When I first arrived as a new employee, I realized 50 percent of the personnel were predicting the island would close within five to ten years. The other half said it would stay open forever. I was quite concerned about this controversial subject and had doubts about staying on the island. After a concerted effort on my part, the United States Customs Service, Treasury Department, took an interest in my availability. It took me over a year to finally persuade the Customs service to allow me to make a lateral transfer from the Department of Justice to the United States Customs Service under the Treasury Department. A letter was sent to Warden Swope requesting his approval for me to make this lateral transfer. He called me into his office and told me I was a very good officer and the government had spent a lot of money training me. In time, I would become a Lieutenant. He flatly refused to grant my request and sent a letter to the Treasury Department demanding they stop trying to hire his officers. I begged for his approval because Alcatraz was potentially going to close, and I would be subject to working and living somewhere other than San Francisco. As a native of San Francisco, I had no desire to live or work anyplace but the city.

During the years 1955 to 1961, Paul Joseph Madigan was Warden. He was the complete opposite of Warden Swope. He was liked by all custodial personnel and had a more pleasant style of leadership. He had worked himself up through the ranks, including Lieutenant, Captain, Associate Warden, and ultimately Warden at Alcatraz. I remember he abolished the bread-and-water diet served while inmates were in isolation. In lieu of bread and water, inmates in isolation were given a diet that consisted of leftovers that were pureed and served in a paper cup. Warden Paul Madigan was a devout Catholic and would attend Mass with the inmates in the prison chapel. The inmates nicknamed him "Promising Paul" because he was always making promises to them. I approached Mr. Madigan in regards to my transfer to Customs, and he told me that he was going to make two lieutenants in the next sixty days. He promised that if I stayed, he would make me a Lieutenant. Unfortunately, the Bureau of Prisons had a policy that promotion to Lieutenant required an automatic transfer to another institution. I did decline the offer. He then said he would approve my transfer to Customs if it could be arranged. It took two more years before I was able to leave in 1957 and transfer into the United States Customs Service. I worked in Customs for thirty-six more years. Including my US Navy time, Alcatraz years, and customs service, I retired with forty-six years of Federal service.

Photo Wardens Paul Madigan and Edward B. Slope
standing in front of photo of President Eisenhower.

CHAPTER 21

A LASTING IMPRESSION

In 1951, two FBI agents came to Alcatraz and went straight to the Warden's office. I was very surprised when they arrested and handcuffed two of my fellow officers and escorted them off the island. This made a lasting impression on me. Later, we all found out that they were bringing mail from the inmates to be mailed in San Francisco and receiving cash in return from the families. As a result, I was always conservative with inmates. I can recall two inmates, John Paul Chase (#238), former public enemy number one, and Steve Sorrentino (#803), a bank robber, who incidentally was born and raised in the same North Beach San Francisco neighborhood as I was. Both inmates asked me questions about my family and people we both knew. I adhered to the strict policy of not divulging anything personal to the inmates and did not answer any of their questions or make any comments.

This subject was thoroughly taught to all trainees on a daily basis. Once you did a favor for an inmate, he had something on you and could eventually force you to further his cause. The only solution for an officer who found himself in this position was to resign and leave the prison service completely.

The two Officers pleaded guilty and received five year sentences each. You can only imagine what could have happened to them if this went further and they smuggled guns into Alcatraz.

CHAPTER 22

AN UNUSUAL ALCATRAZ INCIDENT
INMATE RAY NELSON BRUINSMA, #795

I remember this particular day very well. I was working on the dock with eight inmates. Officer Pehl was in charge. It was a very hot and humid day, around 80 degrees. The inmates were unloading all the cargo from the water barge onto the dock. Inmate Bruinsma, dripping wet with perspiration, jokingly said to Officer Pehl, "It would be great to jump in the bay and have a little swim." To my surprise, Officer Pehl asked me to accompany him and Inmate Bruinsma to the far end of the dock where no one, including the dock tower officer could see. He instructed Inmate Bruinsma to remove his outer clothing, and he then let him jump into the bay and take a ten-minute swim close to the rocks on the end of the island. I was very surprised to see this and wondered what would happen if someone else witnessed this and reported us to a higher authority. It only lasted about ten minutes, and the inmate was told to get out of the water, get dressed, and return to the dock area where the other inmates were working. Officer Pehl, a highly regarded officer, was someone everyone liked, and I thoroughly enjoyed working with him the eight years I was on Alcatraz. I doubted this had ever happened before and doubted it would ever happen again. Believe me; it surely did! I have never mentioned this before, and only now after all these years, I am revealing it in my book. I had some doubts about including this episode in my book, but after over fifty years, no one really cares, but looking back now, I often wonder why Officer Pehl allowed this to happen. I thought it was a very kind gesture on his part to grant this wish for Bruinsma. We didn't worry about Bruinsma escaping because there was nowhere for him to go.

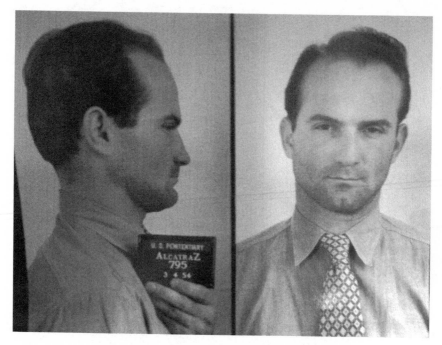

Inmate Ray Nelson Bruinsma #795

CHAPTER 23

ESCAPE ATTEMPT

In 1947, Inmate Floyd P. Wilson (#956) was originally given the death sentence for murder by electrocution. His attorneys appealed the verdict, and President Harry Truman commuted the death sentence to life in prison. Wilson was transferred to Atlanta Penitentiary in Georgia. While in Atlanta, he was in the process of acquiring equipment for an escape attempt. Due to his long sentence, he was transferred to Alcatraz, arriving on January 6, 1952. I remember Inmate Wilson very well. He never gave anyone any trouble, was a loner, never associated with other inmates, and used to stay in his cell reading all the time.

On July 23, 1956, Inmate Wilson was working on the dock. He had disappeared completely by the time a count was attempted at 3:30 p.m. An alarm was sounded, and all the escape procedures were put into effect immediately. The FBI, San Francisco Police, US Coast Guard, and Presidio Military Police were all alerted. Inmate Wilson, taking advantage of all the work activity going on in the dock area, was able to crawl under a fence at the east end of the dock and work himself around the water's edge where he apparently found a cave where he concealed himself. The water and currents surrounding Alcatraz had always been an obstacle and deterrent. Apparently, Wilson had second thoughts or could not find any wood to make a raft. Two Alcatraz officers found him early the next morning against a rock. He was wet and, I would say, glad to be found.

On this particular day, I had the day off and was visiting my mother at her home in San Francisco. Around 5:00 p.m., I received a phone call from the Control Center on Alcatraz to inform me two FBI agents would pick me up and I was to stay with them until further notice. Apparently, they thought because I knew Wilson personally, he could be walking around the Fisherman's Wharf area and I would be able to identify him. The three of us drove all around the waterfront piers and dock areas, from Fisherman's Wharf to the Golden Gate Bridge. We were up all night looking for Inmate Wilson. Looking at Alcatraz from San Francisco, we could see all the activity taking place on the island. The Alcatraz launch, and a US Coast Guard vessel, was circling the island, and all the lights were on all over the island. It meant that they were still looking for him. I believe we received a radio call around 5:00 a.m. informing us that Wilson had been apprehended. I was then driven back to my Mother's house by two F B I agents and enjoyed a good Italian meal.

Inmate Floyd Wilson # 596

CHAPTER 24

EDWARD R. MORROW

On May 3, 1957, the Edward R. Morrow TV program, *Person to Person*, "Life on the Rock," was scheduled to be filmed on Alcatraz. Three workers from his production team arrived a few days before to set up the all the necessary equipment prior to filming the show. Mr. Morrow was the predecessor to broadcasters like Charles Kuralt, Dan Rather, Ted Koppel, Diane Sawyer, and Walter Conkrite. He was by far the leading reporter doing documentaries on radio and television in the 1950s. Each week, he selected a famous person or place to profile on his show *Person to Person*.

The show's format included a personal interview of Warden Madigan by Mr. Morrow in the main gate leading into the cell house. The program's focus was the island and included a tour of Warren Madigan's residence and introduced his wife, Mrs. Madigan. Guess who was the officer working in the main gate? I felt fortunate to be there the day this was scheduled on Alcatraz.

We practiced a few times with Mr. Morrow watching us in New York. As we rehearsed, Mr. Morrow corrected us a few times in order to make it more presentable for national television. When Warden Madigan came into the main gate, Mr. Morrow told me to really slam the door hard so the audience could feel the impact of what it was like to hear those heavy doors slam upon entering the cell house. The show taping proceeded for ten minutes. I was told to look busy at my desk. Later that same evening, Mr. Madigan invited me and a few other officers to his home for coffee and dessert while we watched "Life on the Rock" on television. The program went over very well, and I have the show on my own DVD.

Edward R. Morrow

CHAPTER 25

CELL HOUSE DISTURBANCE

I will never forget one incident that occurred when I first started working at Alcatraz. I was in my apartment in the bachelor's quarters in A Building. The inmates in the cell house were creating a very loud disturbance that could be heard all over the residential area during the course of the night. It was new for me, for I had never experienced anything like that before. The inmates were protesting a kitchen and work area strike and involving many who were in sympathy with them.

At 0800, when I reported to work on the day shift, I was so surprised when we entered the cell house. It looked like a war zone. All the floors had about one to two inches of water on them, and there were clothes, blankets, bedding, wood shelves, and towels strewn all over the place. The inmates had set fires and thrown them out of their cells. Officers had to pull out fire hoses to extinguish the fires. Some inmates removed all the water in their toilet bowls and set a fire in the bowl, which cracked the lining. The inmates proceeded to break up the bowls into small pieces. As we walked into the cell house, we had to walk under the second tier of cells because the inmates would throw pieces of porcelain at us that could do serious damage to us if we got hit by the flying debris!

This severe action was rather stupid on their part because as each cell was inventoried, we could readily see who had done what and how much property damage they did.

The inmates would be transported to D Block for extended periods of time, lose their good time they had built up over a long period of time, and still have to pay for the physical damage they did.

Not all inmates would participate in a disturbance like this; many were trying to behave themselves so they could justify a transfer from Alcatraz to another institution.

This was a very interesting day. I shall never forget it!

Interior of the Cell House

CHAPTER 26

WAXY GORDON AZ #A-1: THE BEER BARON OF NEW YORK

Waxy Gordon, was born Irving Wexler. He was an American gangster who specialized in bootlegging and illegal gambling, He was born to Polish Jewish immigrant parents in New York's Lower East Side on January 19, 1888. Gordon became known as a pickpocket and sneaky thief as a child, becoming so successful he earned the nickname "Waxey" for supposedly being so skilled in picking pockets it was as if his victims' wallets were lined with wax.

One morning in May 1952 /Alcatraz received a phone call from the US Marshalls office that we had to send a special boat trip to pick up Waxey Gordon who was then called the Beer Baron of New York. I was working as the boat officer so away we went to San Francisco to pick him up from the two Marshalls who had him in custody. I was surprised when we took possession of him as he was about 5 feet 5 inches tall and looked like he weighed over 200 pounds. When we arrived back to the island we had to drive him up to the prison in a small truck that I was driving. He was so overweight and unable to navigate a step up, I had to get behind him and give him a good push so we could get him into the back of the truck.

Waxey started young as a pick-pocketer and did time in New York, Boston, and Philadelphia. He was also confined in Sing Sing prison for two years for assault and robbery. In 1934 Waxey was sent to prison for 10 years for income tax evasion. During the prohibition era Waxey became very powerfully involved in the beer business and was a major bootlegger in New York and New Jersey. At one time he owned eight breweries doing a very large illegal business making around two million dollars a year.

During the Second World War Waxey became involved in the black market of sugar rationing and received a year in prison. Soon after the war was over he graduated to narcotics and was apprehended selling drugs to undercover agents and sent to Sing Sing prison for 25 years to life. When arrested in New York in August, 1951, he fell to his knees on a New York street sobbing. "Please kill me-shoot me I am an old man-I will die in prison". He was sent to San Francisco to testify in another narcotics charge. While waiting to testify in the trial he was sent to Alcatraz for safekeeping. Because he was not going to be a permanent inmate at Alcatraz, he was given the temporary number of AZ#A-1

Waxey's health condition was poor and he was suffering from a heart condition so he was assigned to the prison hospital upon arrival at Alcatraz. A few weeks later I was talking to him while he was in the hospital and he told me since he had been on Alcatraz he was getting proper medication, resting, and sleeping well and was feeling much better.

On June 24, 1952 he suffered a heart attack and died at the age of 64.

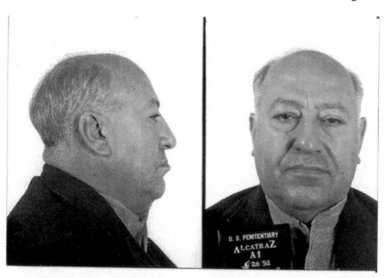

Waxy Gordon AZ # A-1

CHAPTER 27

PRISONERS DAILY ROUTINES

06:30 Bell Rings-----Wake Up call.

06:50: First official count, and all inmates stand up facing cell doors as officers walk by and count all inmates. When count is approved breakfast commences.

0700: Doors open one tier at a time to control flow into Mess Hall. 20 minutes allowed for breakfast.

0730: Inmates assigned to work are let out of cells to march out of cell house to yard and line up in assigned workshop area.

11:30: Work stops, inmates march up to yard and return to cells in cell house.

12:00: Official count is completed and lunch commences. After lunch each day, official sick call is permitted for all who care to attend.

13:45 Work details let out for work as per morning.

16:15: Work stops and inmates return to cells for dinner.

17:00 Dinner is started and final count is completed at 5:30.

20:00 Count by cell house officer in cells.

2100: Lights out

2400: Count by Lieutenants and cell house officers.

0300: Count in Cells.

0500: Count in Cells.

CHAPTER 28

JOHN PAUL CHASE #238
PUBLIC ENEMY #1
PARTNER OF BABY FACE NELSON

John Paul Chase was born on December 26, 1901 and was an American bank robber and Depression-era outlaw. He was a longtime criminal associate of the Karpis-Barker Gang and most notably Baby Face Nelson who later brought him into the John Dillinger gang. FBI Director J. Edgar Hoover once referred to Chase as a "rat with a patriotic-sounding name". Chase and Nelson continued to rob banks with John Dillinger until Dillinger's death in July 1934. After the death of Nelson in November of 1934, Chase fled back to California where he was arrested a month later on December 27, 1934. Chase was sent to Alcatraz where he became one of the longest serving inmates: (March 31, 1935 – September 21, 1954). John Paul Chase was born in San Francisco. He left grade school to work on a ranch and later as an assistant machinist in a railroad yard. He was fired from the railroad job and spent the next few years as a bootlegger in Sausalito, San Rafael, and San Francisco but was not involved in major crime until his association with Baby Face Nelson in the early 1930's, possibly in March 1932.

On October 23, 1933, he and Nelson robbed their first bank together in Brainerd, Minnesota escaping with $32,000. Along the way they picked up a number of other outlaws including Charles Fisher, Tommy Carroll and Homer Van Meter. By March 1934, Nelson had joined John Dillinger's gang although Chase did not participate in their first holdup that month in Sioux Falls, South Dakota. Chase spent much of his time as a "gopher" for Nelson while the gang was in the Chicago area. Among his errands were picking up take-out meals, acquiring weapons and ammunition, and running messages between Nelson and Dillinger. His relatively minor status within the gang was possibly the reason he was not present at the shootout with the FBI when federal agents raided the Little Bohemia Lodge near Manitowish Waters, Wisconsin on April 22.

Chase's first confirmed robbery with the Dillinger gang occurred on June 30, 1934, when he joined Dillinger, Nelson, Van Meter, and two others. They robbed a bank in South Bend Indiana and got $29,890.00. This was a disappointing amount considering the gang's past bank heists and, to make matters worse, a local police officer was killed during their getaway. Dillinger and Van Meter were killed by the FBI during the next two months and Chase fled with Nelson back to Reno for awhile. They eventually returned to Chicago where, on November 26, they stole a car and drove to Wisconsin to stay in one of their safe houses. Upon finding federal agents staking out their hideout however, they turned back to Illinois where they ran into an FBI ambush while driving near Barrington Illinois the next day. Nelson was mortally wounded during the gun battle, however he managed to kill agents Samuel Fowley and Herman "Ed" Hollis before dying of his wounds, allowing Chase to escape.

Chase was later arrested on December 27 by police at Mount Shasta, California while working at a state fish hatchery and extradited to Chicago. He was the first man to be charged under a recently passed law making it a federal crime to kill a federal agent. On March 24, 1935, Chase was tried and convicted for the murder of agent Sam Cowley and sentenced to life imprisonment. At the end of the year, he was officially sent to Alcatraz on March 31, 1935.

Father Clark, the prison's Catholic chaplain, first got him interested in painting. At one point during his stay, the prison had an art instructor who came over from San Francisco to teach the formal techniques of painting. He made a famous painting of a boat, the "J.P. Chase" leaving for San Francisco, with the viewpoint being from the island. He had paintings displayed in the prison and small art galleries, and often sold them.

In September 1954, Chase was transferred to Leavenworth where his second appeal for parole was once again rejected due to Hoover's efforts. He remained in prison for another decade before he was finally released on parole, despite Hoover. Chase moved back to the Bay Area and worked as a custodian at St. Joseph's College, a Catholic Seminary in Mountain View California. His brother was a retired San Francisco police officer and while Chase was on parole he spent most of his free time in San Francisco with his brother.

Chase wanted a presidential clemency but was not able to attain this probably because he was under a lifetime parole.

He died at Stanford University Hospital from cancer on October 5, 1973.

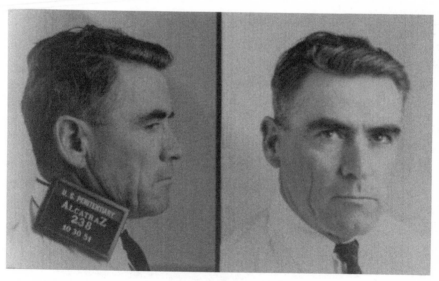

Inmate John Paul Chase #238

CHAPTER 29

TOMOYA KAWAKITA #1059
JAPANESE AMERICAN TURNED TRAITOR
NICKNAME "MEAT BALL"

Alcatraz inmate Kawakita #1059 was born in Calexico, California on September 26, 1921. His parents were both Japanese.

Upon his eighteenth birthday his father brought him to Japan to visit his grandfather with a United States Passport. Upon arrival in Japan he registered with the American Consul and took an oath of allegiance and stayed in Japan while his father returned to the United States.

While in Japan, Kawakita entered Maiyi University and took courses in military training and completed his studies in 1943. While at the university, he was registered as an alien by the Japanese police.

During World War 11, Kawakita worked in a POW camp starting in August of 1943 and managed 400 POW workers, many of whom survived the Bataan Death March. He earned the title "efficiency expert" by his bosses because he was so good at inflicting pain on the prisoners. He tortured many of the Americans who were in this camp in Kyoto, Japan. This POW camp he managed forced the GI's into heavy labor at a Nickel mine. One POW was forced to carry a heavy log up a slope and sustained a severe back injury. Kawakita waited 5 hours to call for medical help causing much suffering to the American POW. He forced the men to beat each other and work in the mine when they were sick and emaciated from lack of nourishment and

85

rest. He slapped one POW whom he overheard calling him a son-of-a bitch in Spanish. He kicked another prisoner named Toland who was ill and hit others who were ill. Daily he would tell them "we will kill all you prisoners anyway, whether you win the war or lose it".

When the war ended in 1945, and the Japanese surrendered on August 10, , he went to the United States Consul in Japan and applied for an American citizenship and when he completed the application he stated he was a United States citizen.

Army veteran William L. Bruce, survivor of Corregidor, the Batann death march and three years in a Japanese prisoner of war camp, couldn't believe his eyes as he shopped with his bride one autumn day in 1946 at the Sears department store in Boyle Heights.

Standing a few aisles away amid the crush of shoppers in that quintessentially American setting was the man responsible for brutalizing Bruce and scores of other GI's held captive in Japan's Oeyama prison camp.

"I was so dumbfounded, I just halted in my tracks and stared at him as he hurried by", Bruce then 24 and attending college under the GI Bill, said shortly after the encounter. "It was a good thing, too," said the former artilleryman. "If I'd reacted then, I'm not sure but that I might have taken the law into my own hands—and probably Kawakita's neck." Instead, Bruce followed him outside the store, jotted down the license plate number of his car and notified the FBI.

Kawakita, who had returned to the United States after the war and enrolled at USC, was tried and convicted of treason in the United States District Court in Los Angeles and sentenced to death on September 2, 1948. More than a dozen POW's testified against him. He was convicted of treason because he was an American citizen.

Kawakita appealed the decision to the United States Supreme Court, which heard his case in April 1952. On June 2, 1952 the Supreme Court ruled to support the lower courts judgment and confirmed Kawakita's death sentence. He was transferred to San Quentin to be put to death in the gas chamber.

On October 29, 1953 President Dwight D. Eisenhower reviewed his punishment as excessive and commuted his sentence to life imprisonment. San Quentin is a California state prison and Kawakita was a federal prisoner doing a federal life sentence so he was sent to Alcatraz.

Ten years later during the closing of Alcatraz prison where Kawakita was serving his time, President John F. Kennedy pardoned him on October 24, 1963 after serving 16 years behind bars on the condition he be deported to Japan and banned him from American soil for life.

During my years on Alcatraz it was difficult for me to even look at this inmate because I served in the Pacific theater while in the Navy. He never gave me any trouble and was nicknamed "meatball" while in Alcatraz. To this day I cannot recall why he had this nickname!

Now more than half a century since his trial, Kawakita holds the distinction of being the last person prosecuted for treason against the United States.

CHAPTER 30

SOME INTERESTING FACTS ABOUT ALCATRAZ

- The first people to visit this rock island may have been native Ohlone and Miwok tribesman, arriving by canoe to gather fresh eggs from the sea birds.

- The Spanish explorers traveling by land originally sighted a 'great bay' in 1769 yet, it would take six long years for their sea-faring counterparts to disover the often foggy and narrow gateway.

- That obscurity would end in 1850, when the U.S. Government surveyors designated Alcatraz Island for defensive fortification and, as an ideal location for a lighthouse, which would begin guiding weary mariners through the rocky and treacherous inlet in 1854.

- In 1859, Fortress Alcatraz became the first U.S. military fortress on the West Coast protecting the San Francisco port and the vast wealth created by California's historic 'Gold Rush'.

- Alcatraz was a military prison from the Civil War era until 1934. Military prisoners built many of the buildings, including the cell house.

- A federal prison , known as the 'big stick' against crime for twenty-nine years from 1934 until 1963, it housed approximately 1,545 prisoners, at about 250 at a time. The worst of the worst were sent to Alcatraz.

- Only 1 percent of the entire federal prison population was housed there. The prisoners at Alcatraz were men who were transferred because of poor behavior in other federal prisons. After doing 'good time', you could go back to a regular Penitentiary.

- The average age of a prisoner was approximately thirty years; the length of stay was usually about five.

- Many had been in prisons or reform schools since their teens. Most were of average intelligence; a few were mentally retarded, and others were quite intelligent. Many had dropped out of school by age fifteen.

- Most were federal prisoners with convictions for federal crimes—kidnapping, bank robbery, income tax evasion, draft violations, post office robbery, et cetera. Some were state or military prisoners housed at Alcatraz for excessive behavioral problems in those prisons.

- Only a handful were famous; among them were Al Capone, "Doc" Barker, "Machine Gun" Kelly, Robert "Bird Man" Stroud, "Ol Creepy" Karpis, and Mickey Cohen.

- There were fourteen escape attempts involving thirty-six men. Thirty-one were brought back dead or alive, and five were never seen or heard from again. Six were shot and killed during their escape attempt, two drowned, twenty three were caught.

- Alcatraz Island also housed staff members and their families. It had a civilian population of about two hundred, approximately seventy-five of whom were children.

- Inmates were entitled to food, clothing, shelter, and medical attention—anything else was a privilege. When an inmate first arrived at Alcatraz, he was furnished a booklet consisting of twenty pages of rules and regulations. It was required to be kept in their cell at all times and consisted of fifty-three specific rules all inmates had to follow to the letter.

- When I first started as an officer on Alcatraz, my starting salary was three thousand per year.

- Although the salary was small, there were many benefits, such as free uniforms, which were cleaned and pressed at no charge, and bed linens, which were washed and pressed, as well as free shoe repairs.
- An apartment in the officers' bachelor's quarters was nine dollars per month. After three months, I received a letter notifying me it had been raised to eleven dollars a month.
- Officers eating in the officer's dining room paid twenty-five cents a meal. When I received my pay, I went to the accounting office and purchased meal tickets for two weeks.
- Alcatraz Dining Hall was referred to as the Mess Hall. It is a long wing on the west end of the Main Cell house situated in the center of the island. It is connected to the block by a corridor known as "Times Square" as it passes beneath a large clock approaching the entrance way to the dining hall. In addition, most people are not aware as they entered the mess hall above their heads are fourteen large canisters which contained live tear gas. In the event of a major disturbance, the officer in the gun cage on the exterior of the wall of the dining room had the ability to pull a lever which would release the gas after receiving permission from the control center. These canisters are still there today but are usually overlooked by visitors unless pointed out by the park rangers during a tour.
- Alcatraz was well-known for having the best food within the federal prison system. The original Alcatraz menu was established in 1934. Disturbances in prisons were commonly caused by bad food. Alcatraz authorities knew food quality was important and therefore provided good food.
- A typical meal for breakfast consisted of oatmeal, cornflakes, milk, dried fruit, sweet rolls, toast, and coffee.
- A typical meal for lunch was hamburgers, fried potatoes, a vegetable, cake, and coffee.
- A typical meal for dinner was assorted meats, mashed potatoes, gravy, vegetables, bread, dessert, and coffee.

- Inmates were permitted to eat as much as they liked within 20 minutes, provided they left no wasted food. Waste would be reported and may make the prisoner subject to removal of their privileges' if they made a habit of it.

- Meals on holidays and Sundays consisted of a traditional dinner (e.g., Thanksgiving and Christmas). A special food item was always added.

- On Christmas Day (only), each inmate was given a gift bag that included cigarettes, cigars, and candy.

- Inmates assigned to B Block shaved on Mondays, Wednesdays, and Fridays. Inmates assigned to C Block shaved on Tuesdays, Thursdays, and Saturdays. The cell house officer on the 4pm to 12 pm midnight shift, passed out blades to each inmate. They had three hours to complete shaving and had to surrender the blades back to the officer. No beards, mustache, side burns, or facial hair was allowed. If an inmate refused to shave he was placed in solitary confinement and "forced shaved" with a dry razor by the officers in D block. Each inmate was provided with a shaving mug, shaving brush, soap, and nail clippers. They were required to shower twice a week.

- Alcatraz is an island surrounded by salt water, but the island itself does not have its own fresh-water supply. To this day, water is delivered in five-gallon containers and is a continuous problem.

- All the water, food, and other supplies used on Alcatraz had to be transported to the island by a huge water barge two and three times a week.

- The water transported to the island was primarily used to do the laundry in the industry area of the prison. The prisoners did all the laundry for the military installations in the entire bay area.

- I believe in 1953 or 1954, each cell on Alcatraz, excluding D Block, was wired for two outlets so inmates could listen to two radio programs. The choices consisted of shows such as Shirley Temple or Hopalong Cassidy and sports programs. Each cell had headphones for the inmates to use.

- Inmates could play string instruments in their cells between 7:00 and 8:00 p.m. They were not allowed to play percussion instruments, as this was considered the "quiet hour."

- Building #64, the large facility you see as you approach the island, was used primarily for the people who lived on Alcatraz. It had a small Mom and Pop shop, and it was run for the convenience of the island residents. The store was managed by a correctional officer and his wife.

- When I initially arrived on Alcatraz, there were twelve roundtrip boat trips per day. Later, this was expanded to fourteen per day.

- In emergency situations, extra boat trips were provided.

- Today, Alcatraz remains a bird sanctuary; however, the sea gulls are the most numerous species, and they drive the average person who walks around the island crazy.

- The name Alcatraz means "pelican." It originated with the Spanish explorer Lieutenant Juan Manuel de Ayala. He was the first person to map San Francisco Bay and Alcatraz

- For many, the island represents a myriad of mixed images, mystery, intrigues, crime and punishment...a fabled destination offering a concrete and stone reality for infamous legends and Hollywood movies.

- Alcatraz is an island-monument to layers of American history as well as a contemporary parkland surprisingly rich in wildlife and nature and a special place with many stories to share.

- Alcatraz Island is protected, in part, as the landmark site for the first US Light Station, and military fortress, to be constructed on the west coast and to protect the island's indigenous and abundant sea-birds.

- The formidable Main Prison Building still stands, beckoning the curious, yet now surrounded in stark contrast by restored historic gardens, and wild flora advancing over the ruins of previous inhabitants.

- Park Rangers, Conservancy interpreters, and Volunteers conduct a wide range of educational and interpretive programs sharing the island's unique geography and it's special place in history.
- After a long and significant history lighting the way to the West, protecting a grand harbor, confining the dangerous, and confronting the past, Alcatraz Island is continually being renovated and restored, readied to welcome a future full of curious new visitors.

CHAPTER 31

RESPONSIBILITIES OF BEING A CORRECTIONAL OFFICER ON ALCATRAZ

Most tours of for correctional officers duty consisted of three straight months at one position. They had two or three specialized positions, which required replacing officers who were on sick leave and annual leave. On any given eight am to five pm shift there were about thirty five to forty officers on duty. On the four pm to twelve midnight shift there were fourteen officers.

There were four strategically located towers throughout the island as follows:

Dock Tower, Road Tower, Hill Tower, and Model Tower.

The Dock Tower and Road Tower were manned three hundred sixty five days a year, twenty- four hours a day. The two remaining towers, Hill Tower and Model Tower, were maintained within the framework of the Industries normal working hours.

The Road Tower observed the San Francisco side of Alcatraz. That officer's function was to control the Sally Port directly below that led into the Industry's area. That tower had the ability to oversee the whole industry area that was facing the bay which was vitally important for custodial purposes. This was very vulnerable for escapes. Directly below the Road Tower, an inmate gardener, maintained a fully landscaped and beautiful hillside garden. This inmate was under the direct supervision of the Road Tower officer.

The Cell House had an East end and West end Gun Gallery maintained by officers.

There were officers assigned in the Cell House at the following posts;, , Cell House, D Block, Hospital, Kitchen, and Clothing Room.

Alcatraz had a large Industries program consisting of laundry, furniture shop, cobbler shop, glove shop, tailor shop, and manufacturing of Navy cargo nets. There were custodians (guards) who were in charge of and supervising these various shops. They were overseen by the Lieutenant in the work areas and were under the direct supervision of the Towers in the Industry area.

My least favorite job was the Yard Wall Officer position. It was often cold and windy on the island and I had to wear an overcoat that weighed about twenty pounds. Although the coat was extremely heavy it kept me warm while carrying a .38 caliber revolver, and a 30 caliber Army carbine rifle.

The most interesting tower for me was the Dock Tower directly above where the Warden Johnson boat docked. This tower supervised the inmates working on the dock, all the passengers arriving and departing, and the dock comprised of continuous activity at all times. One of the responsibilities of the Dock Tower officer was to make sure pleasure boats stayed beyond the buoys, which were 200 yards away from Alcatraz. If they got too close I had to yell on the Bull Horn and warn them to stay back! One of the important functions of the Dock Tower officer was to make sure the inmates working on the dock were lined up behind the yellow line where he could count them before the officer lowered the key to the boat operator preparing for departure.

The Hill Tower was maintained by an officer, during inmates working hours in the Industry area. This tower sat up on a hill which looked down on the entire work area and controlled a Sally-Port for vehicles and personnel entering and leaving the Industry area.

The Model Tower sat on top of the Model building at the extreme West end of Alcatraz at the waters edge where you could see and observe the entire Industries area.

In conclusion, I remember in inmate by the name Steve Sorrentino, an Italian, who came from North Beach. He worked in the Cobbler area and asked me how I liked my shoes done. I told him just ordinary soles and heels. He said "I will take care of you". He not only repaired my shoes, but he gave me full soles instead of half soles, new shoe laces, and they were returned to me very highly polished! I think he was trying to tell me something.

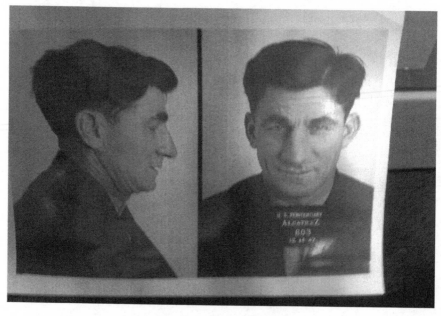

Inmate Steve Sorrentino #803

CHAPTER 32

GUIDELINES FOR VISITORS

Rules and Regulations were strictly enforced and conversations were closely monitored. It was the duty of each correctional officer to make sure visitors understood and were completely aware of the following directives. Failure to comply would result in the termination of the visit and could result in revocation of any or all future visitation privileges for yourself and prisoner in question.

1. Physical contact is prohibited, and your visit will be conducted through the Visitation windows only.

2. Conversations are monitored, and subjects discussed will be limited to family matters including health, finances, recent births and deaths, and future visit dates.

3. Conversations relating to the internal affairs or operating procedures of this institution or discussions pertaining to other prisoners are not permitted.

4. Immediate family were allowed to visit which included Mother, Father, Sister, Brother and Adult children.

5. Visits were allowed 1 to 2 hours.

6. Family were not allowed to bring any gifts but could donate money to the inmates personal fund for incidentals.

7. Many of the inmates came from the East and Mid-West and their families could not visit due to the distance and financial constraints. They were able to send letters to the inmates but the letters were also kept to a minimum.

8. Inmates were allowed two outgoing letters a week and could receive seven incoming letters a week.

9. During holidays such as Mother's Day, Christmas Day, Easter, Father's Day and birthdays inmates were allowed to send and receive more letters.

This book could not be completed without the valued cooperation of the following:

Mark DeVincenzi
Nancy DeVincenzi
Michael Esslinger, Alcatraz Author and Historian
John Martini, Alcatraz Historian
Jolene Babyak, Alcatraz Author
John Cantwell, Park Ranger
George Durgerian, Park Ranger
Robert Luke, Former Alcatraz Inmate #1118
Ian Craig, Video Photographer
Tim Brazil, Video Photographer

Special Thank you:
National Archives and Records, San Bruno, California
Hornblower Cruises, San Francisco, Californina

Testimonials

"George DeVincenzi is truly a part of the Rock's amazing history. His first-hand stories about Alcatraz are both fascinating and harrowing. With incredible detail and insight, he brings to life his experiences working in America's toughest penitentiary".
--John A. Martini
Retired National Park Ranger and Historian
Author, *Alcatraz at War and Fortress Alcatraz*

"George and I were in Alcatraz at the same time, but on different sides of the bars. I never had any animosity toward any guard, and never understood any prisoner who did. The guards time at Alcatraz was just as regulated as the prisoners. For the last

three years we have been working together giving lectures and talks to the Alcatraz visitors and have become good friends."
Robert Luke #1118AZ Former Alcatraz Inmate
Incarcerated for 5 years.

" At long last, the book we've been waiting for...with precise prose and vividly written accounts, George brings us face-to –face with some of America's most infamous criminals! An insightful memoir offering a rare insideinside view of life behind the hidden walls of Alcatraz".
Michael Esslinger, Author: A definitive History of the Penitentiary Years

"George is one of the few guards who remembers everything! If you want to know whar really happened on Alcatraz...read this book".
Gennifer Choldenko
Author of: Al Capone Does My Shirts

EPILOGUE

Little did I know at the time, when I first worked on Alcatraz, that my experiences would prepare me and lay the foundation for a long career in the United States Customs Service. The law enforcement activities and responsibilities were very similar to what I was doing on Alcatraz.

When I transferred to customs from Alcatraz, my entry-level position was a Customs Port Patrol Officer GS 5. My duties consisted of shaking down crewmembers who were exiting various foreign and US arriving vessels. I was checking them for contraband, drugs, and different smuggled items. I did this for four years.

In 1961, I was promoted to United States Customs Inspector, GS 7. In one year, I was promoted to a GS 9. I worked at this grade for twelve years, and I was then promoted to a Supervisory GS 12 inspector. My experiences included working at the United States Customs House, San Francisco Waterfront, San Francisco Airport, Oakland Airport, and the Oakland Waterfront. I was also in charge of the Ports of Stockton, Richmond, and Alameda.

Looking back after all these years, I often compare working on Alcatraz to the United States Customs Service. The best way I can express this is "I went from hell to heaven." Altogether, I retired with forty-five years of service for the Federal government.

Made in the USA
San Bernardino, CA
23 June 2017